Financial Rocket
FREEDOM BEFORE AGE 30
• Build Wealth Early
• Create Passive Income
• Achieve Financial Freedom
YASH D.

FINANCIAL ROCKET - FREEDOM BEFORE AGE 30

First edition. February 22, 2026.

ISBN: 979-8232286101

Written by Yash d..

Table of Contents

To every young dreamer who refuses to settle for average.

To those who choose discipline over distraction, growth over comfort, and freedom over fear.

May this book be the spark that launches your financial rocket — and may you build the courage to chase freedom before age 30.

Your journey starts now.

PREFACE

The Race Is Real. But So Is Your Advantage.

If you are holding this book, you are already different.

Most people talk about wanting money. Few decide to understand it. Even fewer build a structured plan to control it.

Look around.

Everyone is busy. Everyone is earning. Everyone is spending. But very few are building real freedom.

The world is running for money.

But almost no one is being taught how to make money run for them.

This book was written for that gap.

Not for dreamers who want shortcuts.

Not for gamblers chasing trends.

Not for people waiting for luck.

This book is for builders.

It is for the 22-year-old who just got their first salary and does not want to repeat the financial mistakes they saw growing up.

It is for the 25-year-old who feels stuck despite earning well.

It is for the ambitious professional who knows that salary alone will not create freedom.

It is for anyone under 30 who refuses to be financially average.

Because here is the truth no one tells you early enough:

Income does not create wealth.

Discipline does.

And another truth:

Time is your biggest unfair advantage right now.

If you learn how to manage, multiply, and protect money in your twenties, you compress decades of struggle into a few focused years.

That is what this book is about.

Not theory.

Not complicated financial jargon.

Not unrealistic "get rich quick" promises.

This is a practical blueprint.

Everything inside these pages is structured to move you step by step:

From confusion to clarity.

From salary dependency to asset ownership.

From financial stress to financial control.

You will learn how to:

Eliminate debt without feeling trapped.

Build emergency stability that protects your future.

Invest simply and intelligently without fear.

Create side income streams from scratch.

Scale a skill into a business.

Design a lifestyle aligned with your goals.

Build assets that generate passive income.

And most importantly, create a five-year freedom plan that is realistic and achievable.

There is no magic here.

There is mathematics.

There is mindset.

There is momentum.

And there is discipline.

Financial freedom before 30 is not about becoming a billionaire.

It is about reaching a point where:

Your investments pay a portion of your expenses.

You can leave a toxic job without panic.

You can support your family without stress.

You can choose opportunities based on growth, not desperation.

That is real freedom.

The earlier you build it, the stronger your life becomes.

Many people in their forties wish they had started at 23.

You are not late.

You are early.

And that is powerful.

Let me be honest with you.

There will be moments when saving feels boring.

Moments when investing feels slow.

Moments when friends upgrade lifestyles faster than you.

Moments when discipline feels uncomfortable.

But five years from now, the gap between you and the average person will be dramatic.

Because while others consumed, you built.

While others reacted, you planned.

While others chased, you compounded.

This book does not promise overnight success.

It promises a clear system.

If you follow the system consistently, the results are inevitable.

You do not need a finance degree.

You do not need rich parents.

You do not need perfect timing.

You need:

A decision.

A plan.

Execution.

Every chapter you are about to read connects like parts of a rocket.

Mindset is the fuel.

Income is the engine.

Investments are the boosters.

Protection is the shield.

Discipline is the navigation system.

When all of them align, lift-off is not optional.

It is guaranteed.

The next five years will pass whether you act or not.

The only difference will be your net worth, your confidence, and your freedom.

You can remain dependent on salary cycles.

Or you can build assets that work while you sleep.

You can keep guessing.

Or you can follow a blueprint.

The choice begins now.

Take this seriously.

Read slowly.

Implement aggressively.

Revisit chapters.

Track your progress.

And most importantly, commit to finishing what you start.

Because the person you become in this journey matters more than the money you earn.

By the time you reach the final page, I do not want you to feel motivated.

I want you to feel equipped.

Ready.

Clear.

Focused.

Financial freedom before 30 is not impossible.

It is uncommon.

And uncommon belongs to those who decide.

Welcome to your launchpad.

Your financial rocket is ready.

Now it is time to take control of your future.

Launchpad: The 30-Under-30 Money Mindset

Money Is a Tool, Not a Trophy

Before we talk about investing, side hustles, or passive income, we need to reset something fundamental. Most people treat money as a status symbol. They chase it to impress others, compare themselves constantly, and attach their self-worth to their bank balance. That mindset quietly destroys financial freedom.

Money is not a trophy. It is a tool.

A tool has only one purpose: to help you build something. A hammer builds a house. A laptop builds skills and income. Money builds options.

When you see money as a tool, three powerful shifts happen. First, you stop chasing appearance and start chasing control. Second, you stop spending to impress and start spending to improve. Third, you begin asking a better question: "What can this money build for me?"

If you are under 30, you are sitting on your greatest financial asset. It is not your savings account. It is not your degree. It is time.

Time allows compounding. Time allows skill stacking. Time allows mistakes without permanent damage.

Imagine two people. Aditi starts investing ₹5,000 per month at age 22. Rahul starts investing ₹10,000 per month at age 32. Even though Rahul invests double, Aditi may still end up ahead because of ten extra years of compounding. The lesson is simple: early action beats higher income later.

Financial freedom before 30 is not about becoming a billionaire. It is about building enough assets and income streams so that your life choices are not controlled by fear.

The Freedom Definition

Before you chase freedom, define it.

For some people, freedom means quitting a toxic job. For others, it means supporting their parents without stress. For someone else, it means working remotely from anywhere in the world.

Write your personal definition of financial freedom in one sentence. Not a fantasy. A measurable outcome.

For example:

"I want ₹50,000 per month coming from investments and side income by age 30."

"I want zero debt and one year of expenses saved."

"I want the ability to take a six-month break without financial panic."

This clarity matters. Without it, you will chase random goals. With it, every financial decision becomes easier.

If you earn ₹40,000 per month and spend ₹35,000, your freedom number is not mysterious. If you reduce expenses to ₹30,000 and build assets generating ₹30,000 per month, you are financially independent at your current lifestyle.

Freedom is math. Not motivation.

The First Mental Model: Control the Gap

The gap between what you earn and what you spend is your power zone.

If you earn ₹50,000 and spend ₹48,000, your gap is ₹2,000. If you earn ₹50,000 and spend ₹30,000, your gap is ₹20,000. That gap is what builds wealth.

Most people focus only on income. Smart people focus on the gap.

Early in your career, you may not control your salary completely. But you always control part of your spending. Increasing the gap gives you speed.

Example. Two friends, Sameer and Kunal, both earn ₹60,000 per month. Sameer spends ₹55,000 and invests ₹5,000. Kunal spends ₹40,000 and invests ₹20,000. After five years, assuming a reasonable 12 percent annual return, Kunal's portfolio will be dramatically larger. The difference is not talent. It is the size of the gap.

Your first mission in your 20s is simple: widen the gap aggressively and intelligently.

The Second Mental Model: Skills First, Assets Next

In your 20s, your best investment is not always the stock market. It is your skill stack.

If you can increase your income from ₹30,000 to ₹80,000 within five years because of high-value skills, that impact is larger than chasing small investment returns.

Think of skills as income multipliers. Coding, digital marketing, sales, video editing, financial analysis, communication, AI tools, negotiation. These skills are leverage.

For example, Riya learns performance marketing and starts freelancing in the evenings. Within a year, she adds ₹25,000 per month to her income. That additional cash, invested monthly, accelerates her wealth far more than trying to optimize a ₹3,000 SIP.

Your 20s are for aggressive skill acquisition. Allocate time every week to learn something that increases earning power.

A practical formula that works:

Forty hours per week for your job.

Ten hours per week for skill growth.

Five hours per week for income experiments.

Even if only one experiment succeeds, your financial trajectory changes permanently.

The Third Mental Model: Small Systems Beat Big Intentions

Most people say they want to save money. Very few build systems to save automatically.

Intentions fail. Systems win.

If you wait until the end of the month to see what is left, nothing will be left. Instead, reverse the order. On the day your salary arrives, immediately transfer a fixed percentage to investments or a separate account.

For example, if you earn ₹45,000, automate ₹9,000 into a recurring investment. Live on the remaining ₹36,000. You will adjust. Humans adapt faster than they think.

This is called paying yourself first.

Another system that works is a weekly money review. Every Sunday evening, spend 20 minutes reviewing expenses, income, and progress toward your goal. It prevents financial drift.

Wealth is built through boring consistency.

The Fourth Mental Model: Lifestyle Inflation Is the Silent Killer

As income increases, expenses naturally rise. Better phone, better car, better apartment. There is nothing wrong with upgrading your life. The danger comes when every income increase is matched by equal spending increase.

If your salary jumps from ₹40,000 to ₹70,000 and your expenses jump from ₹35,000 to ₹65,000, your financial life has not improved much.

Instead, practice partial lifestyle upgrades.

When your income increases, allocate at least 50 percent of the raise toward investments. If you get a ₹20,000 raise, invest ₹10,000 and enjoy the remaining ₹10,000.

This habit alone can cut years off your freedom timeline.

The Fifth Mental Model: Income Streams Create Stability

Relying on one income source is risky. Jobs are not permanent. Markets change. Companies restructure.

Building a second stream does not require quitting your job. It requires creativity and consistency.

Examples that work in real life include tutoring online, content creation, freelance services, small digital products, affiliate marketing, or part-time consulting.

Arjun worked as a software developer earning ₹80,000 per month. On weekends, he built a simple course teaching beginners how to crack coding interviews. Within a year, it generated ₹25,000 monthly. That second stream reduced his fear of job loss and increased his investment capacity.

The goal is not exhaustion. The goal is optionality.

Facing Fear and Social Pressure

Your biggest financial enemy may not be inflation. It may be social comparison.

Friends buying expensive bikes. Colleagues upgrading phones every year. Social media showing luxury lifestyles.

If you measure success by appearance, you will sabotage your freedom.

Adopt a different identity. Instead of saying, "I want to look rich," say, "I am building assets."

When others spend on liabilities, you accumulate investments. The gap widens silently. Five years later, the difference becomes visible.

There is quiet power in delayed gratification.

Practical Exercise: Your 30-Day Financial Reset

For the next 30 days, follow this plan strictly.

Track every expense. Not roughly. Exactly.

Cut one recurring unnecessary expense.

Increase income by at least ₹3,000 through any small side task.

Automate at least 10 percent of income into savings or investments.

Read or watch educational content about money for 15 minutes daily.

At the end of 30 days, compare your financial awareness and bank balance to before. The psychological shift alone will motivate you.

Redefining Rich

Rich is not owning luxury brands. Rich is having control over your calendar.

Rich is being able to say no to toxic environments.

Rich is helping your family without panic.

Rich is having investments that work while you sleep.

When you redefine rich, your behavior changes.

The Long Game

Financial freedom before 30 does not mean you will stop working at 30. It means you will work by choice, not desperation.

The path is not glamorous. It is structured.

Increase income.

Control expenses.

Automate investments.

Build assets.

Repeat.

Most people underestimate what they can achieve in ten focused years. If you start at 20 and stay disciplined until 30, the compounding effect on skills, money, and confidence is extraordinary.

This chapter is your launchpad. Not hype. Not fantasy. A structured way of thinking about money.

From here onward in this book, every strategy, tactic, and framework will build on these mental models. The gap. Skills first. Systems over intentions. Controlled lifestyle inflation. Multiple income streams. Long-term thinking.

You do not need luck. You need clarity and execution.

If you commit to the mindset in this chapter, financial freedom before 30 stops being a dream and starts becoming a calculated target.

And calculated targets are achievable.

Your Financial GPS: Net Worth, Cashflow, and Goals

Why You Need a Financial GPS

If Chapter 1 was about mindset, this chapter is about measurement.

Imagine getting into a car and saying, "I want to go somewhere successful." Without a destination and a map, you will waste fuel and time. That is how most people handle money. They work hard, earn, spend, maybe save something, but they do not know exactly where they are or where they are heading.

Your Financial GPS has three coordinates: Net Worth, Cashflow, and Goals.

Net worth tells you where you stand today.

Cashflow tells you how money moves every month.

Goals tell you where you are going.

When you combine these three, financial confusion disappears. Decisions become mathematical instead of emotional.

Understanding Net Worth in Simple Terms

Net worth is not complicated. It is one equation:

Total Assets minus Total Liabilities equals Net Worth.

Assets are things that put money in your pocket or hold financial value. Savings account balance, investments, fixed deposits, mutual funds, stocks, gold, business value.

Liabilities are what you owe. Credit card dues, personal loans, education loans, vehicle loans.

Example.

Ankit has:

Savings: ₹80,000

Mutual funds: ₹1,20,000

Laptop resale value: ₹20,000

Total assets: ₹2,20,000

He also has:

Education loan: ₹1,50,000

Credit card outstanding: ₹30,000

Total liabilities: ₹1,80,000

Net worth equals ₹40,000.

Now imagine Meera has ₹50,000 savings and no debt. Her net worth is ₹50,000. Even though Ankit earns more, Meera is financially stronger at this moment.

Net worth removes illusions.

Many people focus only on salary. But salary without net worth growth is like running on a treadmill. You feel active but you are not moving forward.

Your first action today is to calculate your exact net worth. Not approximately. Exactly.

How to Track Net Worth Monthly

Create a simple spreadsheet or notebook page with these columns:

Date

Total Assets

Total Liabilities

Net Worth

Update it once every month on the same date.

The number may not grow fast in the beginning. That is normal. What matters is direction. If it increases steadily over 12 months, you are on the right path.

Even if you start with negative net worth because of student loans, tracking gives clarity. Suppose your net worth is minus ₹3,00,000 today. After six months, it becomes minus ₹2,40,000. That is progress. You are moving toward zero. That is momentum.

What gets measured improves.

Cashflow: The Real Engine

Net worth is your position. Cashflow is your engine.

Cashflow is the difference between what you earn and what you spend every month.

Income minus expenses equals monthly surplus or deficit.

If income is ₹60,000 and expenses are ₹45,000, your surplus is ₹15,000. That ₹15,000 is your wealth-building fuel.

If income is ₹60,000 and expenses are ₹62,000, you are running a deficit. Even with a decent salary, you are going backward.

Track cashflow weekly for at least three months. Write down every rupee spent. Food delivery, subscriptions, transport, random online shopping. Awareness alone reduces waste.

Many people discover they are leaking ₹3,000 to ₹8,000 per month in small, unconscious expenses.

That money, if invested at 12 percent annually for ten years, can grow into several lakhs. Small leaks sink big ships.

The Three Expense Buckets

To simplify cashflow, divide expenses into three categories:

Essentials

Growth

Lifestyle

Essentials include rent, groceries, utilities, transport. These are necessary for survival and stability.

Growth includes investments, skill courses, books, business expenses.

Lifestyle includes eating out, entertainment, gadgets, vacations.

If your essentials are consuming 80 percent of income, you have limited flexibility. Consider optimizing rent, transportation, or shared living arrangements.

If lifestyle is consuming more than growth, it is time to rebalance.

A practical starting ratio for someone under 30:

Essentials 50 to 60 percent

Growth 20 to 30 percent

Lifestyle 10 to 20 percent

These are guidelines, not rigid rules. Adjust according to your income level.

The 90-Day Target System

Long-term goals are important. But they often feel distant. The brain responds better to short, intense missions.

That is why you will operate in 90-day cycles.

Ninety days is long enough to see results and short enough to maintain urgency.

Step One: Choose One Primary Financial Goal

Not three. Not five. One.

Examples:

Increase monthly income by ₹10,000.

Pay off ₹50,000 credit card debt.

Build ₹1,00,000 emergency fund.

Invest ₹60,000 in 90 days.

Clarity increases execution.

Step Two: Break It into Monthly Targets

If your 90-day goal is ₹60,000 investment, that means ₹20,000 per month. If income does not allow it, you must either cut expenses or increase income.

This is where creativity begins.

Step Three: Weekly Actions

If your goal is income growth, weekly actions might include:

Applying to three freelance gigs.

Building one small portfolio project.

Contacting five potential clients.

If your goal is debt payoff:

Selling unused items.

Negotiating interest rate.

Redirecting bonuses toward repayment.

Progress happens weekly, not magically at day 90.

Example of a 90-Day Sprint

Rahul earns ₹45,000 per month and saves only ₹5,000. He decides his 90-day goal is to build a ₹75,000 emergency fund.

He currently has ₹20,000 saved. He needs ₹55,000 more.

He calculates:

If he saves ₹15,000 per month, in three months he will reach ₹65,000, combined with existing ₹20,000 equals ₹85,000.

To free up ₹10,000 extra per month, he moves to shared accommodation saving ₹6,000. He cancels two subscriptions saving ₹1,500. He takes weekend tutoring earning ₹4,000 per month.

In 90 days, he reaches the target.

What changed? Not his salary. His decisions.

Creating Your Personal Financial Dashboard

Your dashboard should have five numbers visible at all times:

Current Net Worth

Monthly Income

Monthly Expenses

Monthly Investment Amount

90-Day Goal Progress

Review this dashboard every Sunday evening.

Ask three questions:

Did my net worth increase this month?

Is my surplus growing?

Am I on track for my 90-day goal?

If the answer is no, adjust immediately. Do not wait for the end of the year.

Financial drift is dangerous because it feels comfortable.

Setting SMART Money Goals

Vague goals fail. Specific goals succeed.

Instead of saying, "I want to save more," say, "I will invest ₹12,000 every month for the next three months."

Instead of saying, "I want to earn more," say, "I will generate ₹15,000 from freelance design work by June 30."

Attach numbers and deadlines.

Your brain works better with measurable targets.

Emergency Fund: Your First Safety Checkpoint

Before aggressive investing, build a basic emergency fund.

Minimum target: three months of essential expenses.

If your essentials are ₹25,000 per month, your emergency fund target is ₹75,000.

Keep it in a safe, liquid account. This fund is not for vacations or gadgets. It is for job loss, medical emergencies, or urgent repairs.

An emergency fund reduces anxiety. When anxiety reduces, decision-making improves.

Tracking Progress Without Obsession

Tracking is powerful. Obsession is harmful.

Do not check stock prices daily. Do not panic during short-term market drops.

Your focus in your 20s should be contribution consistency, not daily valuation.

Invest monthly. Increase skills. Grow income.

Let compounding do its work.

Common Mistakes to Avoid

Ignoring small debts because they feel manageable. Small debts accumulate interest quietly.

Depending on bonuses to meet goals. Bonuses are uncertain.

Copying someone else's financial plan without adjusting to your income and lifestyle.

Skipping tracking because numbers feel uncomfortable.

Discomfort is temporary. Ignorance is expensive.

The Compounding Effect of Clarity

When you track net worth monthly for five years, something powerful happens. You start seeing patterns. You understand how lifestyle changes affect savings. You see how side income accelerates growth. You notice how debt slows you down.

This awareness builds confidence.

And confidence leads to bigger decisions.

Investing more aggressively. Starting a small business. Negotiating salary without fear.

Clarity compounds just like money.

Your First Assignment

Before moving to the next chapter, complete these actions:

Calculate your exact net worth.

Track your expenses for 30 days.

Define one 90-day financial target.

Set up automatic investment or savings transfer.

Create a simple financial dashboard.

Do not skip this step.

Mindset without measurement is motivation without movement.

Your Financial GPS is now installed.

From here forward, every strategy in this book will plug into these numbers. Your net worth will rise. Your surplus will grow. Your goals will become sharper.

Financial freedom before 30 is not luck.

It is direction plus disciplined execution.

Now you have direction.

Bootstrapping Income: Side Hustles That Scale

Why Side Income Is No Longer Optional

Relying on one income source in your 20s is financially fragile. Jobs change. Companies restructure. Markets fluctuate. Inflation rises silently. If your only strategy is "wait for annual increment," your growth will always be limited by someone else's decision.

Side income is not about greed. It is about control.

When you build even one additional stream of income, three things happen. Your financial stress reduces. Your savings rate increases. Your confidence grows.

The best part is this: you do not need capital to begin. You need skill, effort, and structured execution.

This chapter gives you eight practical side-income blueprints that require zero or near-zero investment. These are not fantasies. They are repeatable models. If you apply them seriously for 90 days, at least one can become a meaningful income stream.

Before we begin, understand one rule. Start small. Scale later. Proof of concept is more important than perfection.

Blueprint 1: Skill-Based Freelancing

If you have any usable skill, you already have income potential.

Writing, video editing, coding, graphic design, social media management, basic accounting, resume writing, translation, tutoring. The market is huge.

Step one is clarity. Identify one skill you can deliver at beginner level within seven days.

Step two is packaging. Instead of saying, "I do graphic design," say, "I create Instagram post designs for small businesses at ₹1,500 for 10 posts."

Specific offers sell faster.

Step three is outreach. Contact 20 small businesses directly through email or social media. Offer a free sample or discounted first project. Your goal is your first paying client, not maximum profit.

Example.

Neha knew basic Canva design. She created three sample Instagram posts for a local bakery and sent them as a demo. The bakery paid her ₹2,000 for a monthly package. Within four months, she had five clients earning ₹15,000 per month working evenings.

Zero capital. Only initiative.

To scale, increase prices gradually and specialize in one niche. Specialists earn more than generalists.

Blueprint 2: Micro Tutoring and Knowledge Monetization

You do not need to be a professor to teach. If you are one step ahead of someone, you can guide them.

Students in class 11 can teach class 9. Engineering graduates can coach coding basics. English speakers can train spoken English. Finance students can teach basic investing.

Start with one topic and one clear outcome.

Instead of saying, "I teach math," say, "I help class 10 students score 85 percent plus in algebra."

Offer small group sessions online. Even five students paying ₹2,000 per month equals ₹10,000 income.

Example.

Aman prepared for competitive exams. While preparing, he started weekend doubt-solving sessions for juniors at ₹1,500 per student. Within six months, he earned enough to cover his living expenses.

Scaling path includes recorded courses, digital notes, or membership groups.

Blueprint 3: Service Arbitrage

Service arbitrage means you act as a bridge between clients and skilled freelancers.

Suppose you find a small business that needs website design for ₹25,000. You hire a capable freelancer for ₹18,000 and manage the project. Your margin is ₹7,000.

Your skill here is coordination and client communication.

Start small. Offer website setup, social media management, video editing packages, or SEO basics.

The key is building a small network of reliable freelancers.

Example.

Rohit had strong communication skills but limited technical skills. He found two freelance developers and partnered with them. Within one year, he managed projects worth ₹8 lakh, earning commissions without writing a single line of code.

Zero capital. Only negotiation and organization.

Blueprint 4: Digital Products with Minimal Tools

Digital products require time, not money.

Ebooks, templates, planners, Notion dashboards, resume templates, social media caption packs, exam preparation notes.

If you have solved a problem for yourself, you can package that solution.

Start simple. Create a 20-page PDF solving one specific issue.

Example.

Priya cracked a competitive internship process. She documented her preparation strategy and created a ₹299 guide. She shared it in relevant student groups. Even selling 100 copies per month generates ₹29,900.

Scaling happens through bundling, upselling, or launching advanced versions.

Focus on clarity and practical value. Do not overcomplicate design.

Blueprint 5: Content Creation with Monetization Intent

Content creation is not about going viral randomly. It is about building authority in a niche.

Choose one topic: finance for students, fitness for beginners, coding tutorials, productivity tips.

Post consistently three to five times per week.

Initially, income will not come from ads. It will come from services, consulting, or affiliate products.

Example.

Karan started posting simple investing explainers. After six months, he built trust. He partnered with a financial platform and earned commission per referral. He also sold a beginner investing workshop at ₹999.

Income grows when trust grows.

Treat content like a business asset, not entertainment.

Blueprint 6: High-Demand Local Services

Not every side hustle is online.

Local services can scale surprisingly fast. Examples include:

Laptop cleaning and repair.

Home deep cleaning coordination.

Fitness coaching in parks.

Event photography.

Moving and packing assistance coordination.

Start by identifying one problem people frequently complain about.

Example.

Sahil noticed many hostel students struggled with laundry during exams. He organized a pickup and drop laundry service partnering with a local vendor. He added a ₹10 per kg margin. With 40 regular users, his monthly income crossed ₹20,000.

The opportunity is everywhere if you observe.

Blueprint 7: Reselling and Flipping

Flipping means buying undervalued items and selling at higher price.

Start with items you understand: books, electronics, furniture, bikes.

Scan online marketplaces for underpriced listings. Improve presentation, take better photos, and resell.

Example.

Megha bought used study tables from students moving out of hostels at ₹1,000 each. She cleaned and resold them at ₹2,000. Selling 15 tables in a month generated ₹15,000 profit.

Capital requirement is small and reinvested quickly.

The skill here is spotting price inefficiencies.

Blueprint 8: Skill Stacking and Consulting

Skill stacking means combining two basic skills to create unique value.

For example:

Coding plus communication equals technical trainer.

Finance plus design equals financial content creator.

Fitness plus marketing equals online coaching brand.

If you work in a job already, ask what problems your company faces repeatedly. Learn to solve one of those deeply.

Example.

An HR executive learned basic data analysis. She started offering employee engagement analytics consulting to startups. Within a year, she earned more from consulting than her salary.

The future belongs to those who combine skills creatively.

How to Choose the Right Blueprint

Do not try all eight at once.

Ask three questions:

What skill do I already have at beginner level?

What problem do I understand personally?

Which option can I test within seven days?

Pick one. Commit for 90 days.

If it fails, analyze and switch. But give it structured effort before quitting.

The Zero-Capital Execution Plan

Week 1

Choose blueprint. Define specific offer. Identify target customer.

Week 2

Create basic portfolio or sample. Start outreach to at least 20 potential customers.

Week 3

Close first paying client or sale. Focus on delivery quality. Collect testimonial.

Week 4 to 12

Refine pricing. Improve offer. Increase outreach volume. Track income weekly.

By the end of 90 days, you should know whether this stream can scale.

Scaling Principles

Increase price as skills improve.

Standardize delivery process.

Automate repetitive tasks.

Build repeat customers instead of chasing new ones constantly.

Scaling does not mean working 16 hours daily. It means improving efficiency and pricing power.

Common Mistakes in Side Hustles

Waiting until you feel fully ready.

Underpricing permanently without raising rates.

Jumping between ideas every week.

Ignoring customer feedback.

Spending money on branding before validating demand.

Focus on revenue first. A simple document and basic communication are enough to start.

The Confidence Effect

When your first ₹5,000 arrives from a side hustle, something changes internally. You realize income is not limited to salary. You understand that value exchange creates money.

That realization is powerful.

Even if the amount is small, it proves a concept. From there, scaling becomes a strategic exercise, not a dream.

Income as a Multiplier for Freedom

Remember Chapter 2. Cashflow is your engine. Side income increases surplus. Surplus increases investments. Investments increase net worth.

Everything connects.

If you add ₹15,000 monthly through side work and invest it consistently for eight years at reasonable returns, you could build a portfolio worth several lakhs. That portfolio reduces dependence on a single paycheck.

Bootstrapping income is not about hustle culture. It is about accelerating freedom.

You do not need investors. You do not need a big office. You do not need family wealth.

You need structured action.

Choose one blueprint. Execute for 90 days. Track results. Improve.

That is how side hustles scale.

And that is how your financial rocket gains thrust.

Compound Power: Investing for Beginners

Why Investing Is the Real Wealth Engine

Earning money is important. Saving money is powerful. But investing money is transformational.

If income is the fuel and savings is the storage tank, investing is the engine that multiplies everything.

Most people delay investing because they think they need a large amount to start. That belief is expensive. Investing rewards time more than amount. The earlier you begin, the more powerful compounding becomes.

Compounding simply means earning returns on your returns.

If you invest ₹1,00,000 at 12 percent annual return, after one year you have ₹1,12,000. In the second year, you earn 12 percent not just on ₹1,00,000 but on ₹1,12,000. That extra ₹12,000 also starts generating returns. Over years, this effect accelerates dramatically.

The earlier you activate compounding, the easier financial freedom becomes.

The Investor Identity Shift

Before learning tools, adopt the identity of an investor.

An investor thinks long term. An investor does not panic over short-term fluctuations. An investor focuses on consistent contributions.

Do not approach investing as gambling. Do not chase hot tips from friends. Do not try to predict markets daily.

Your advantage as a young investor is time and regular contribution. That is enough.

Understanding Asset Allocation

Asset allocation means dividing your investments across different asset classes to manage risk and growth.

The three primary categories for beginners are:

Equity

Debt

Cash

Equity includes stocks and equity mutual funds. They offer higher potential returns but fluctuate in the short term.

Debt includes bonds, debt mutual funds, fixed deposits. They offer stability but lower returns.

Cash includes savings accounts and emergency funds. It offers liquidity but minimal growth.

A simple allocation rule for someone under 30 is:

Seventy to eighty percent in equity.

Ten to twenty percent in debt.

Rest in cash for emergencies.

This is not fixed. Adjust based on risk tolerance. If market drops make you panic, reduce equity slightly.

The key is balance.

Index Funds: The Simplest Entry Point

You do not need to pick individual stocks to build wealth.

Index funds are mutual funds that track a market index like Nifty 50 or Sensex. Instead of betting on one company, you own small portions of many top companies.

Why index funds are powerful:

Low cost.

Diversification.

Long-term market growth participation.

Minimal management effort.

Historically, broad market indices have delivered solid long-term returns over decades despite short-term volatility.

Example.

If you invest ₹10,000 per month in a low-cost index fund for 10 years at an average 12 percent return, your total investment of ₹12,00,000 could grow to around ₹23,00,000 or more. The growth is not linear. It accelerates in later years due to compounding.

The earlier you begin, the stronger the compounding curve.

Understanding SIP: Systematic Investment Plan

SIP stands for Systematic Investment Plan. It allows you to invest a fixed amount every month into a mutual fund.

SIP removes timing stress. You do not need to worry whether the market is high or low. You invest consistently.

When markets fall, your fixed amount buys more units. When markets rise, it buys fewer units. Over time, this averages out the cost. This process is called rupee cost averaging.

Suppose you invest ₹5,000 every month.

In month one, NAV is ₹50, you buy 100 units.

In month two, NAV falls to ₹40, you buy 125 units.

In month three, NAV rises to ₹60, you buy 83 units.

Over time, this disciplined investing smooths volatility.

SIP builds habit. Habit builds wealth.

The Emergency Fund Before Aggressive Investing

Before investing heavily in equity, build an emergency fund.

Minimum target: three to six months of essential expenses.

If your monthly essentials are ₹30,000, aim for ₹90,000 to ₹1,80,000 in liquid savings.

Why this matters:

If the market falls and you lose your job at the same time, you should not be forced to withdraw investments at a loss.

Emergency funds protect investments.

Protection is part of smart investing.

Understanding Risk and Volatility

Risk is not market fluctuation. Real risk is permanent loss of capital.

Market volatility is normal. Over long periods, markets trend upward despite temporary declines.

For example, during economic crises, markets may drop 20 to 40 percent. Investors who panic and sell lock in losses. Investors who stay invested often recover as markets rebound.

If you invest with a 10 to 15 year mindset, short-term volatility becomes less frightening.

Your goal is not to avoid every drop. Your goal is to survive and stay invested.

Tax-Smart Investing Basics

Taxes reduce returns if ignored.

In India, equity investments held longer than one year qualify for long-term capital gains tax at favorable rates compared to short-term trades.

Short-term trading increases tax burden and stress.

Using tax-advantaged options such as ELSS funds under Section 80C can reduce taxable income while building investments.

Example.

If you invest ₹1,50,000 annually in eligible instruments under 80C, you reduce taxable income by the same amount. For someone in the 20 percent tax bracket, that means saving ₹30,000 in taxes while building assets.

Tax planning is not about avoiding taxes illegally. It is about using available provisions wisely.

The Power of Increasing SIP Annually

One of the simplest wealth accelerators is increasing your SIP every year.

If you start with ₹5,000 per month at age 23 and increase it by just ₹1,000 every year, by age 30 you could be investing ₹12,000 monthly.

This gradual increase aligns with salary growth and avoids lifestyle shock.

Example.

Year 1: ₹5,000 per month

Year 2: ₹6,000 per month

Year 3: ₹7,000 per month

Continue this pattern. The difference after 10 years compared to fixed ₹5,000 investment can be substantial.

Small annual increases create massive long-term impact.

Avoiding Common Beginner Mistakes

Chasing highest past returns without understanding risk.

Investing lump sum in hype stocks based on social media tips.

Stopping SIP during market downturns.

Checking portfolio daily and reacting emotionally.

Ignoring expense ratios in mutual funds.

Investing without defined goal.

Investing is simple but not easy. Discipline separates successful investors from frustrated ones.

Goal-Based Investing

Every investment should have a purpose.

Short-term goals like buying a laptop in one year should not be in equity funds. Use safer instruments.

Long-term goals like retirement or financial freedom can be equity-heavy.

Divide goals into categories:

Short term under three years.

Medium term three to seven years.

Long term above seven years.

Match asset allocation accordingly.

Clarity reduces anxiety.

A Simple Starter Allocation Example

Let us assume you earn ₹50,000 per month and can invest ₹10,000 monthly.

Allocation example:

₹7,000 into equity index fund via SIP.

₹2,000 into debt mutual fund or recurring deposit.

₹1,000 into emergency fund until target reached.

As income grows, increase equity and debt proportionally.

Do not overcomplicate. Complexity often reduces action.

Understanding the Long Game

Imagine two people.

Person A invests ₹10,000 monthly from age 22 to 32 and then stops.

Person B starts investing ₹10,000 monthly from age 32 to 42.

Even though both invest for 10 years, Person A may end up with significantly more wealth at retirement because early money had more time to compound.

Time in the market beats timing the market.

If you are in your 20s reading this, you are in a powerful position. Every year you delay costs future wealth.

From Investor to Wealth Builder

Investing is not about getting rich quickly. It is about building assets patiently.

Once you understand allocation, SIP discipline, and tax efficiency, your focus shifts from excitement to execution.

The real growth happens quietly.

Month after month.

Year after year.

Contribution after contribution.

There will be periods when markets fall. There will be headlines predicting doom. Ignore noise.

Stick to your allocation. Increase investment with income growth. Review annually, not daily.

Compounding rewards consistency.

Your Action Plan

Open an investment account if you have not already.

Calculate your emergency fund target and start building it.

Choose one low-cost index fund and begin SIP within the next seven days.

Decide your asset allocation and write it down.

Increase your SIP annually.

Review portfolio once every six months.

That is enough to build strong foundations.

Compound power does not require genius. It requires patience.

When combined with increasing income from side hustles and disciplined tracking from previous chapters, investing becomes the amplifier of your financial rocket.

You earn.

You save.

You invest.

You repeat.

Over time, that repetition turns ordinary income into extraordinary freedom.

Debt Nuke: Strategies to Crush Debt Fast

The Silent Weight of Debt

Debt is not just a financial burden. It is a psychological weight. It reduces confidence, limits risk-taking, and quietly steals future income through interest payments.

Not all debt is evil. An education loan that increases earning potential or a home loan aligned with long-term planning can be strategic. But high-interest consumer debt, especially credit cards and personal loans, is dangerous.

If you want financial freedom before 30, uncontrolled debt must be eliminated aggressively.

Debt is negative compounding. While investments grow over time, debt grows against you. If a credit card charges 36 percent annual interest, that is not a small number. It means the bank is compounding wealth using your money.

This chapter is about destroying that cycle with clarity and strategy.

Step One: Total Debt Clarity

Before attacking debt, list everything.

Create a simple table with:

Lender name

Outstanding amount

Interest rate

Minimum monthly payment

Due date

Most people avoid this step because it feels uncomfortable. But avoidance makes debt stronger.

Example.

Anjali has:

Credit Card A: ₹45,000 at 36 percent interest

Credit Card B: ₹25,000 at 30 percent interest

Personal Loan: ₹1,20,000 at 18 percent interest

Total debt: ₹1,90,000

Once written clearly, the problem becomes structured. Structure allows strategy.

Understanding Interest: The Real Enemy

Interest rate determines how fast debt grows.

If you owe ₹1,00,000 at 36 percent annual interest and make only minimum payments, you could end up paying far more than ₹1,00,000 over time.

High-interest debt above 20 percent must be prioritized. It drains wealth silently.

The faster you eliminate high-interest debt, the faster your financial life stabilizes.

Snowball vs Avalanche Method

There are two proven strategies to eliminate multiple debts.

The Snowball Method

You pay minimum amounts on all debts except the smallest one. You attack the smallest debt aggressively until it is cleared. Then you move to the next smallest.

This method builds psychological momentum. Quick wins create confidence.

Example.

If you have debts of ₹20,000, ₹50,000, and ₹1,00,000, focus on clearing ₹20,000 first, even if its interest rate is slightly lower.

The Avalanche Method

You pay minimum amounts on all debts except the one with the highest interest rate. You attack the highest-interest debt first.

This method saves more money mathematically.

If you have debts at 36 percent, 30 percent, and 18 percent, attack the 36 percent debt first.

Which method is better?

If you are highly disciplined and motivated by numbers, choose avalanche.

If you feel overwhelmed and need quick psychological wins, choose snowball.

The best method is the one you will stick to consistently.

Debt Attack Formula

Once you choose strategy, calculate your total monthly repayment capacity.

Example.

You earn ₹50,000 per month.

Essential expenses are ₹30,000.

Minimum debt payments total ₹8,000.

That leaves ₹12,000 surplus.

Instead of spending that surplus, allocate it entirely toward one target debt.

If you attack ₹45,000 credit card debt with ₹12,000 extra plus minimum payments, you can eliminate it within four months.

After clearing first debt, redirect full payment amount toward next debt.

This creates a debt elimination snowball effect.

Increasing Attack Speed

If you want to crush debt faster, increase surplus temporarily.

For the next 90 days:

Pause non-essential lifestyle expenses.

Sell unused items.

Take small side gigs.

Redirect bonuses and tax refunds.

Example.

Rohan had ₹2,50,000 in mixed debts. He committed to a six-month aggressive plan. He stopped dining out, sold his unused gaming console and bike, and took weekend freelance work. He paid off ₹1,80,000 within six months.

Temporary intensity creates permanent relief.

Refinancing: Lowering the Interest Burden

Refinancing means replacing high-interest debt with lower-interest debt.

For example, converting credit card outstanding of 36 percent into a personal loan at 14 percent significantly reduces interest cost.

Before refinancing, check:

Processing fees

Prepayment penalties

New interest rate

Loan tenure

If overall interest paid reduces meaningfully, refinancing can accelerate debt payoff.

However, refinancing only works if spending behavior changes. Otherwise, you risk accumulating new credit card debt again.

Balance Transfer Strategy

Some banks offer balance transfer options at lower introductory rates.

If managed responsibly, transferring ₹1,00,000 from 36 percent card to a 12 percent promotional offer can reduce interest dramatically.

But discipline is essential. Do not treat freed credit limit as spending power.

Negotiation Scripts That Work

Many people assume interest rates are fixed and non-negotiable. That is not always true.

Banks prefer recovery over default.

If you are struggling, call customer support proactively.

Sample Script for Interest Reduction:

"I have been a customer for several years and have always tried to maintain timely payments. Due to temporary financial stress, I am finding it difficult to manage the current interest rate. I would like to request a review and possible reduction in interest to help me clear the outstanding amount responsibly."

If you have good payment history, some banks may offer reduced rate or structured repayment.

Sample Script for Settlement Discussion:

"I want to close this account and avoid further penalties. I can arrange a lump sum of ₹X within 30 days. Is there a possibility of a one-time settlement or reduced payoff amount?"

Settlement may impact credit score. Use it carefully and as a last option.

Always request written confirmation before making final payment.

Avoiding Future Debt Traps

Crushing debt once is powerful. Staying debt-free is wisdom.

Practical rules:

Do not use credit card for lifestyle upgrades.

Pay full outstanding amount every month.

Keep credit utilization below 30 percent of limit.

Build emergency fund to avoid borrowing during crisis.

If you cannot pay full credit card bill, treat it as emergency.

Credit cards are tools. Misused, they become traps.

Good Debt vs Bad Debt

Not all debt is equal.

Education loans that increase earning potential can be strategic.

Home loans aligned with long-term plan can build asset ownership.

High-interest consumer debt for gadgets, vacations, or impulse purchases is destructive.

Ask before borrowing:

Will this increase my income?

Will this create an asset?

Can I repay within planned timeline without stress?

If answer is no, reconsider.

Psychological Reset After Debt Freedom

The day you clear your last high-interest debt feels powerful.

But the journey does not end there.

Redirect previous EMI amount into investments immediately.

If you were paying ₹15,000 per month toward debt, continue paying ₹15,000 into SIP.

This prevents lifestyle inflation and accelerates wealth building.

Debt repayment builds discipline. Investing builds freedom.

Case Study: From Debt to Asset Builder

Sneha had ₹3,00,000 in credit card and personal loan debt at age 26. Her monthly salary was ₹55,000.

She calculated expenses and reduced them from ₹40,000 to ₹30,000 by shifting to shared housing and cutting subscriptions.

She took freelance writing work earning ₹8,000 per month.

Her total debt repayment capacity became ₹25,000 monthly.

Using avalanche method, she cleared high-interest credit card first in five months. Then attacked personal loan.

Within 14 months, she became debt-free.

Instead of celebrating with lifestyle upgrades, she redirected ₹25,000 monthly into investments.

At 30, she had over ₹12 lakh invested.

The transformation started with one decision: confront debt honestly.

The Debt Nuke Action Plan

List all debts with interest rates.

Choose snowball or avalanche method.

Calculate total monthly repayment capacity.

Increase surplus aggressively for 90 days.

Explore refinancing if beneficial.

Negotiate respectfully where possible.

Redirect EMI into investments after clearance.

Debt elimination is not glamorous. It requires discipline, sacrifice, and short-term discomfort.

But freedom from debt changes your trajectory completely.

Once high-interest debt is gone, your money starts working for you instead of against you.

Your financial rocket cannot lift off while tied down by heavy chains.

Break those chains.

Crush the debt.

Then redirect that power toward building assets that compound in your favor.

Automate and Protect: Banking, Insurance, and Safety Nets

Why Protection Comes Before Acceleration

Before you try to grow money aggressively, you must protect what you have built.

Many people focus only on earning and investing. They ignore risk management. Then one emergency wipes out years of progress.

A medical crisis. A job loss. A family emergency. A market downturn.

Financial freedom before 30 is not only about building wealth fast. It is about building a system that survives shocks.

In this chapter, you will design your financial safety system:

A clean banking structure

A cash buffer

Basic insurance coverage

An emergency action plan

Once this is in place, your financial rocket becomes stable.

The Three-Account Banking System

Simplicity wins. Complexity creates mistakes.

Instead of mixing salary, expenses, savings, and investments in one account, separate them.

Account One: Income Account

Your salary and all income sources are credited here. This account is temporary. Money does not stay here.

Account Two: Expense Account

This account handles all fixed and variable monthly expenses. Rent, groceries, EMIs, subscriptions, utilities.

Transfer a fixed monthly amount from Income Account into Expense Account at the beginning of the month.

Account Three: Wealth Account

This account is for savings and investments. SIPs, long-term savings, emergency fund. This is not touched for lifestyle expenses.

Automation rule:

The day salary hits, automatic transfers move money into Expense and Wealth accounts.

You never rely on willpower.

Example.

Amit earns ₹80,000 monthly.

He structures it like this:

₹40,000 to Expense Account

₹25,000 to Wealth Account

₹15,000 stays temporarily for flexibility and adjustments

Because transfers are automatic, he never accidentally overspends.

Automation reduces decision fatigue. Decision fatigue causes financial mistakes.

The Cash Buffer: Your Shock Absorber

An emergency fund is not optional.

It is your financial shock absorber.

Minimum target: Three months of essential expenses.

Ideal target: Six months of essential expenses.

If your monthly essential expenses are ₹35,000, your minimum buffer is ₹1,05,000. Ideal is ₹2,10,000.

This money should be:

Liquid

Safe

Easily accessible

Keep it in high-interest savings account or liquid mutual fund.

Do not invest emergency funds in stocks. Market volatility and emergencies often arrive together.

Case Example.

Ravi lost his job during a company restructuring. Because he had six months of expenses saved, he did not panic. He searched calmly for a better opportunity and avoided high-interest borrowing.

Without a buffer, he would have used credit cards or borrowed from friends.

Emergency fund protects your dignity.

How to Build the Emergency Fund Fast

If you do not have one, make it priority before aggressive investing.

Step One. Pause extra investments temporarily.

Step Two. Direct full savings toward emergency fund.

Step Three. Use bonuses, incentives, freelance income to accelerate.

Set a 90-day mini goal.

Example.

If your target is ₹1,20,000 and you can save ₹20,000 monthly, you will reach it in six months. If you sell unused items and add ₹30,000 extra, timeline shortens.

Emergency fund building is short-term sacrifice for long-term stability.

Basic Insurance: Protect Income and Assets

Insurance is not investment. It is protection.

Confusing insurance with investment is one of the biggest financial mistakes young earners make.

There are three essential types to consider.

Health Insurance

Medical emergencies can destroy savings.

Even if your employer provides health insurance, consider personal coverage. Job changes can create gaps.

Minimum coverage depends on city and lifestyle, but ₹5–10 lakh individual coverage is common baseline.

Family coverage requires higher amount.

Choose policies with:

Low waiting period

Wide hospital network

Reasonable claim settlement ratio

Health insurance prevents debt during medical crisis.

Term Life Insurance

If someone depends on your income, term insurance is essential.

Term insurance is pure protection. It pays a lump sum if you pass away during policy term.

Do not mix with investment-linked policies.

Coverage rule of thumb: 10–15 times your annual income.

If you earn ₹10 lakh annually, consider ₹1–1.5 crore coverage.

Premium for term insurance at young age is surprisingly affordable.

If you are single with no dependents, you may postpone. But once family depends on you, do not delay.

Disability and Income Protection

Injury or disability can impact earning capacity.

Some employers offer coverage. If not, consider personal accident or disability insurance.

Protecting income is as important as protecting life.

What Not to Buy

Avoid complicated insurance-investment hybrids promising high returns.

Avoid policies you do not understand.

Avoid buying insurance because a friend or relative is selling.

Insurance is about risk transfer, not profit.

The Emergency Playbook

An emergency fund and insurance are defensive layers. But you also need a clear action plan.

When crisis hits, emotions run high. A pre-decided plan prevents panic decisions.

Your emergency playbook should include:

List of emergency contacts

Insurance policy numbers

Nominee details

Bank account information

EMI due dates

Essential monthly expenses list

Keep digital copy and a printed copy accessible.

Discuss basics with a trusted family member.

Example.

Megha maintained a simple document listing accounts, passwords stored securely, insurance details, and investment summary. When her father faced medical emergency, she handled paperwork calmly without confusion.

Preparation reduces chaos.

Automation of Investments and Bills

Late payments damage credit score and create penalties.

Set auto-debit for:

Credit card full payment

EMIs

Insurance premiums

SIPs

Review once every quarter to ensure accuracy.

Automation ensures consistency.

Consistency builds wealth quietly.

Layered Financial Protection Model

Think of your financial life like layers.

Layer One: Cash buffer

Layer Two: Insurance coverage

Layer Three: Low debt

Layer Four: Diversified investments

Without the bottom layers, top layers are unstable.

Do not rush into high-risk investments without completing foundational protection.

Job Loss Scenario Simulation

Ask yourself:

If I lose job tomorrow, what happens?

How many months can I survive without borrowing?

Which expenses can I cut immediately?

Simulate worst-case scenarios mentally.

If you can survive six months comfortably, your stress level reduces dramatically.

Financial security increases career confidence. You can negotiate better salary, switch jobs, or start business without fear.

Protecting Digital and Banking Security

Young earners often ignore digital safety.

Enable two-factor authentication for banking apps.

Do not share OTP or passwords.

Avoid public Wi-Fi for financial transactions.

Regularly check bank statements for unknown charges.

Financial freedom includes protecting against fraud.

Case Study: Protection Before Growth

Karan, age 25, earned ₹60,000 monthly. He was excited about stock investing and cryptocurrency.

Instead of investing entire surplus, he first:

Built ₹2,00,000 emergency fund in eight months.

Purchased ₹10 lakh health insurance.

Bought ₹1 crore term insurance after marriage.

Automated ₹15,000 monthly SIP.

Two years later, he faced temporary job loss. Because of preparation, he continued SIPs without breaking investments.

His friends who had no emergency fund liquidated stocks during market downturn.

Protection preserved compounding.

The Peace of Financial Stability

Money is not only numbers. It is emotional stability.

When you know:

Your expenses are automated

Your emergency fund is ready

Your family is insured

Your bills are on time

You sleep better.

Financial anxiety reduces.

You think long-term.

This chapter may not feel as exciting as investing or side hustles. But it is the foundation.

Without protection, growth collapses under pressure.

Build your buffer.

Automate your system.

Insure wisely.

Prepare for the unexpected.

When storms arrive, you will not panic.

You will stand steady.

And steady rockets travel farther than unstable ones.

Skills That Convert: Learn to Sell Your Time and Product

The Skill Economy Has Replaced the Degree Economy

A degree may open the first door. Skills determine how far you go.

In the modern economy, income is directly connected to the value you can create and communicate. If you can solve a problem that makes or saves someone money, your earning potential increases rapidly.

Financial freedom before 30 is rarely built through salary increments alone. It is built by stacking high-income skills that convert effort into income efficiently.

This chapter will help you identify skills with high return on time, price them correctly, and sell them confidently.

Understanding High-ROI Skills

High-ROI skills share three characteristics:

They solve urgent or expensive problems.

They are measurable in outcomes.

They are scalable or repeatable.

Low-ROI skills consume time but generate limited income growth.

For example, data entry is time-bound and low leverage. Sales funnel design, on the other hand, can directly increase a company's revenue.

Focus on skills that directly impact revenue, cost reduction, or growth.

Five Categories of High-Conversion Skills

Digital Marketing

Businesses constantly need customers. Skills such as social media marketing, paid advertising management, search engine optimization, and email marketing are high demand.

If you can run paid ads that generate ₹5 lakh in revenue, charging ₹40,000 for campaign management becomes logical.

Sales and Negotiation

Sales is the ultimate income multiplier. If you can close deals, your income ceiling rises dramatically.

Learning persuasion, objection handling, and structured pitching allows you to sell services, products, or even your own startup.

Copywriting

Words that convert are valuable. Sales pages, ad copy, email sequences, landing pages all drive revenue.

A skilled copywriter can earn more than a graphic designer because words drive action.

Tech and Automation

Web development, app development, automation scripting, no-code tools, AI integrations. Businesses want efficiency.

If you can save a company 20 hours per week through automation, your value becomes clear.

Content Creation and Personal Branding

Video editing, content strategy, YouTube growth, LinkedIn ghostwriting. Attention is currency.

If you can build audience or grow brand visibility, companies will pay.

How to Choose Your Skill

Choose based on intersection of:

Market demand

Your interest

Learning curve

Income potential

Do not wait for passion clarity. Start with practicality.

Example.

Priya had no technical background but strong communication skills. She learned copywriting through online courses and practice. Within six months, she landed her first ₹15,000 project. Within two years, she was earning ₹1 lakh per month freelancing.

Skill choice does not need perfection. It needs execution.

The 90-Day Skill Acquisition Plan

Month One: Learn

Choose one skill. Study fundamentals daily for 60–90 minutes. Use structured courses and real-world case studies.

Month Two: Practice

Work on mock projects. Offer free or discounted work to build portfolio. Create three sample projects.

Month Three: Monetize

Start pitching. Apply on freelance platforms. Reach out to small businesses. Publish content showcasing expertise.

Consistency over 90 days creates income-ready skill.

Selling Your Time vs Selling Your Product

Selling Time

Freelancing is selling your hours or projects.

Example: Charging ₹2,000 per hour for consulting.

Advantage: Immediate income.

Limitation: Income tied to time.

Selling Product

Creating digital products, templates, courses, automation tools.

Example: Selling a ₹999 resume template downloaded by 500 people.

Advantage: Scalable income.

Limitation: Requires upfront effort.

Begin with selling time. Transition to selling products for scale.

Pricing Strategy for Beginners

Most beginners underprice due to fear.

Instead of charging based on time, charge based on value.

Value-Based Pricing Example

If your service increases a client's monthly revenue by ₹1,00,000, charging ₹25,000 is reasonable.

If you charge ₹3,000 because you feel inexperienced, you limit growth.

Entry-Level Pricing Strategy

Start slightly lower than market average to gain clients quickly. After three successful projects, increase rates by 20–30 percent.

Confidence grows with delivery.

The Minimum Viable Portfolio

You do not need 20 clients to start. You need proof of ability.

Create:

Three case studies

One professional LinkedIn profile

One simple website or portfolio page

Testimonials, even from unpaid projects

Case Study Template

Client Problem

Your Strategy

Execution Steps

Result Measured

Example.

Client: Local gym struggling with membership growth.

Action: Ran targeted social media campaign with limited budget.

Result: 45 new signups in 30 days.

Even small wins build credibility.

Freelancing Outreach Template

Direct Message Template

Hello [Name],

I noticed your business has strong potential but your [specific issue] could be optimized for better results. I specialize in [your skill] and recently helped a similar business achieve [specific result]. I would love to offer a quick audit or discussion to explore opportunities.

This approach works because it is personalized and value-driven.

Cold Email Structure

Subject: Quick Idea to Increase [Business Metric]

Hi [Name],

I came across your company while researching [industry]. I noticed an opportunity to improve [specific issue]. I recently worked on a similar project that achieved [result]. If you are open, I would be happy to share a short strategy outline.

Keep emails short and focused on results.

Handling Objections Confidently

Common Objection: Your price is high

Response:

I understand budget is important. The goal is not cost but return. If this project generates [expected result], the investment becomes justified. Let us focus on outcome.

Common Objection: We need to think

Response:

Of course. May I ask what specific concerns you would like clarity on? I am happy to address them.

Objections are normal. Stay calm. Clarify. Do not panic discount immediately.

Time Management for Skill Income

If you have a job and freelance simultaneously, structure time strictly.

Two hours daily focused deep work.

Weekend delivery slots.

Clear client deadlines.

Avoid overcommitting early. Quality builds reputation.

Transitioning from Freelancer to Specialist

Generalists earn. Specialists earn more.

Instead of being social media manager for everyone, become:

Instagram growth strategist for fitness coaches

LinkedIn ghostwriter for startup founders

Web developer for real estate agents

Narrow focus increases perceived expertise and allows premium pricing.

Case Study: From Zero to ₹80,000 Monthly

Arjun was 23, earning ₹35,000 monthly in job. He learned video editing over 90 days.

He reached out to 50 YouTubers.

Five responded.

Two became paying clients.

Within eight months, he had six clients paying ₹15,000 each per month.

He later created a video editing preset pack and sold it online.

His income crossed ₹80,000 monthly within one year.

Skill plus action created leverage.

Building Reputation Capital

Deliver on time.

Communicate clearly.

Underpromise and overdeliver.

Reputation compounds faster than marketing.

Referrals reduce acquisition effort.

Investing in Skill Growth

Reinvest part of freelance income into:

Advanced courses

Better tools

Networking events

Personal branding

Your skill is your most powerful asset in your twenties.

Unlike market investments, skill investment has unlimited upside.

From Income to Freedom

When you can convert skill into income reliably, fear reduces.

You are no longer dependent on one employer.

You can negotiate salary confidently.

You can build side income streams.

You can pivot careers if necessary.

Skill monetization is control.

Control creates freedom.

In your journey toward financial freedom before 30, income growth through skill stacking is your fuel system.

Master one high-conversion skill.

Sell it confidently.

Price it based on value.

Then scale beyond your time.

That is how your financial rocket accelerates.

Scale: From Side Hustle to Small Business

The Shift From Extra Income to Enterprise

A side hustle pays bills. A business builds assets.

There comes a point when your freelance or side income stops feeling like "extra" and starts showing patterns. Clients repeat. Referrals increase. Revenue becomes predictable. That is the signal to think bigger.

Scaling is not about working more hours. It is about building systems that generate income without your constant presence.

In this chapter, you will learn how to transition from solo operator to structured small business, understand basic legal foundations, set up simple bookkeeping, and create growth loops that multiply revenue.

When to Consider Scaling

Scaling too early creates stress. Scaling too late limits growth.

You are ready to scale when:

You have consistent monthly revenue for at least three to six months.

You are turning down work due to time constraints.

You have repeatable processes.

Demand exceeds your personal capacity.

Example.

Neha was managing social media for four clients. She was fully booked and receiving referrals every month. Instead of rejecting new clients, she hired a junior designer and trained them using her process. Revenue doubled within five months.

Scaling begins when demand meets structure.

Step One: Clarify Your Core Offer

Before building a business, simplify your service.

Do not offer ten different services. Focus on one core outcome.

Instead of "digital marketing services," position as:

Lead generation for real estate agencies.

YouTube growth for educators.

Paid ad management for ecommerce brands.

Clarity attracts better clients and simplifies operations.

Specialization reduces confusion.

Understanding Basic Legal Structures

When income grows, legal structure becomes important. It protects you, builds credibility, and prepares for tax compliance.

Common basic structures include:

Sole Proprietorship

Simple to start. You and business are legally the same entity. Suitable for freelancers and early-stage entrepreneurs.

Partnership

If starting with a co-founder. Responsibilities and profit sharing must be clearly defined.

Private Limited or Corporation

More formal structure. Suitable for scaling businesses, attracting investors, or building long-term enterprise value.

You do not need complex structure on day one. Start simple, upgrade when revenue stabilizes.

Consult a qualified accountant in your country for compliance details. Legal clarity prevents future complications.

Separate Personal and Business Finances

The moment you treat your hustle like a business, open a separate bank account.

Never mix personal and business expenses.

All client payments go to business account.

All business expenses are paid from business account.

You pay yourself a fixed "salary" from business profits.

Example.

If your business earns ₹1,50,000 in a month and expenses are ₹60,000, profit is ₹90,000.

Instead of spending randomly, transfer ₹60,000 as personal income and keep ₹30,000 for business growth and tax.

Separation creates discipline and clarity.

Simple Bookkeeping System

Bookkeeping is not optional. It is the dashboard of your business.

You need to track:

Revenue

Expenses

Profit

Taxes payable

Outstanding invoices

You can start with a simple spreadsheet.

Columns:

Date

Client name

Service

Invoice amount

Payment status

Expense category

Expense amount

Update weekly.

Example.

Arjun ignored bookkeeping in his first year of freelancing. When tax season arrived, he struggled to calculate profits. He paid penalties due to late filing.

In year two, he tracked everything monthly. He saved 25 percent of revenue separately for tax. No stress, no surprises.

Clarity reduces chaos.

Basic Financial Ratios for Small Business

Even if you are not a finance expert, track three numbers.

Gross Margin

Revenue minus direct costs.

If you charge ₹50,000 for a project and spend ₹20,000 on subcontractors, your gross margin is ₹30,000.

Operating Margin

Revenue minus all expenses.

This shows actual profitability.

Client Acquisition Cost

How much you spend to get one new client.

If you spend ₹10,000 on ads and get two clients, cost per client is ₹5,000.

Understanding these numbers helps in smart decisions.

Building Systems Instead of Working Harder

Freelancers think in hours. Business owners think in systems.

Document everything you do.

How you onboard clients.

How you deliver service.

How you collect payments.

How you communicate updates.

Create standard operating procedures.

When process is documented, you can delegate.

Delegation multiplies capacity.

Hiring Your First Team Member

You do not need a large team. Start small.

Hire for repetitive tasks first.

Design work.

Video editing.

Data entry.

Customer support.

Keep high-value tasks such as sales and strategy initially with you.

Example.

Rahul was spending 20 hours weekly on editing. He hired a part-time editor at ₹25,000 monthly. That freed him to focus on acquiring new clients. Revenue increased by ₹1,00,000 in three months.

Hiring should increase revenue, not just reduce workload.

Creating a Growth Loop

Growth loops create continuous expansion.

A simple growth loop looks like this:

Deliver excellent results

Collect testimonials

Showcase case studies

Attract new clients

Reinvest profits into marketing

Deliver even better results

Each loop strengthens the next cycle.

Example.

A freelance consultant completes a project generating 200 leads for a client. He documents results, shares on LinkedIn, attracts inbound inquiries, closes two new clients, reinvests part of profit into paid ads, and scales further.

One successful result creates momentum.

Content as a Growth Engine

In today's world, content builds trust.

Share insights regularly.

Client wins.

Industry analysis.

Educational posts.

Behind-the-scenes processes.

Content positions you as authority.

Authority reduces selling effort.

You move from chasing clients to attracting them.

Pricing for Scale

As demand grows, increase pricing strategically.

If you have full capacity and waiting clients, price is too low.

Raise rates gradually for new clients.

Example.

If you charge ₹30,000 monthly per client and are fully booked, increase to ₹40,000 for next client. Test market response.

Higher pricing filters serious clients and increases margins.

Never scale low-margin chaos.

Tax Awareness and Compliance

As income grows, tax planning becomes important.

Set aside percentage of revenue monthly for taxes.

Keep invoices and receipts organized.

Consult professional annually if needed.

Avoid ignoring taxes. Growth without compliance becomes risky.

Cash Flow Management

Profit is different from cash flow.

You may close ₹5 lakh in contracts but receive payments late.

Always monitor:

Upcoming payments

Recurring expenses

Tax liabilities

Keep at least one to two months of business expenses as buffer.

Cash flow stability ensures survival during slow months.

When to Convert Into Full-Time Business

Consider full-time shift when:

Business income consistently matches or exceeds salary for six months.

You have at least six months personal expenses saved.

Client pipeline remains stable.

Do not jump impulsively. Calculate risk carefully.

Calculated risk builds confidence.

Case Study: Side Hustle to Agency

Simran started as freelance paid ads specialist earning ₹40,000 monthly part-time.

After one year, she built portfolio of six clients.

She registered small business entity.

Opened business bank account.

Hired junior media buyer.

Documented processes.

Within two years, revenue crossed ₹25 lakh annually.

Her transformation was not sudden. It was structured.

Structure creates scalability.

Mindset Shift: Operator to Owner

As a freelancer, you think:

How many hours can I work?

As a business owner, you think:

How can the system produce results without me?

You move from doing to designing.

Designing systems is leverage.

Leverage builds wealth.

Reinvest for Growth

In early business stages, reinvest profits.

Better tools.

Skilled hires.

Marketing campaigns.

Learning upgrades.

Consumption can wait. Expansion builds asset value.

From Income Stream to Asset

A side hustle gives income.

A business gives asset value.

A well-run business can:

Be sold.

Be automated.

Be passed on.

Asset ownership is different from earning.

Scaling transforms effort into enterprise.

You started with one skill.

You sold your time.

You created results.

Now you build systems.

Scaling is the bridge between active income and financial freedom.

Design your business intentionally.

Track your numbers.

Protect legally.

Build growth loops.

That is how your financial rocket moves from launch to sustained orbit.

Lifestyle Design: Spend Like You Mean It

Money Without Meaning Is Emptiness

Earning aggressively and investing intelligently are powerful. But if you do not design how you spend, money can quietly disappear without increasing happiness.

Many people chase financial freedom only to realize they never defined what freedom looks like.

Lifestyle design answers one question clearly:

What is the purpose of your money?

Financial freedom before 30 is not about deprivation. It is about intentional living. It is about spending on what truly matters and eliminating what does not.

This chapter will help you move from random spending to strategic living.

Minimalism Versus Strategic Living

Minimalism is often misunderstood.

Minimalism is not about owning nothing. It is about removing excess that does not add value.

Strategic living goes one step further. It asks:

Which expenses genuinely increase my happiness, growth, or freedom?

You do not need to live in extreme frugality. You need clarity.

Example.

Two friends earn ₹1 lakh per month.

One spends ₹40,000 on frequent dining, gadgets, and impulsive shopping.

The other spends ₹20,000 on travel experiences, books, fitness, and networking.

Five years later, their bank balances may be similar. But their growth, health, and memories will differ significantly.

Spending shapes identity.

The Spend-to-Happiness Mapping Framework

Instead of cutting expenses blindly, map them.

Step One: List Last Three Months of Expenses

Categorize into:

Housing

Food

Transport

Subscriptions

Shopping

Experiences

Learning

Health

Family

Step Two: Rate Each Category on Happiness Score

Give each category a score from 1 to 10 based on how much genuine satisfaction it gives.

Step Three: Compare Cost Versus Happiness

If you spend ₹15,000 monthly on online shopping but rate happiness as 4, that is inefficient spending.

If you spend ₹3,000 on gym and rate happiness as 9, that is high-value spending.

Redirect money from low-happiness areas to high-happiness areas or investments.

This method creates clarity without guilt.

The Lifestyle Inflation Trap

As income grows, expenses grow automatically.

Better phone. Bigger apartment. Frequent vacations. Premium subscriptions.

Lifestyle inflation is subtle. It feels deserved.

The problem is not upgrading life. The problem is upgrading without strategy.

Rule: Increase lifestyle only after increasing investments.

If income rises by ₹20,000, allocate:

₹12,000 to investments

₹8,000 to lifestyle upgrade

This keeps wealth growth ahead of lifestyle growth.

Fixed Cost Discipline

Your biggest expenses usually include:

Rent or housing

Car EMI

Insurance

Utilities

Keep fixed costs manageable.

If fixed expenses consume 70 percent of income, flexibility disappears.

Target: Fixed expenses below 50 percent of income.

Lower fixed costs increase freedom.

A smaller apartment close to work may give more freedom than a large apartment far away with long commute and high rent.

Designing Your Ideal Week

Lifestyle design is not only about money. It is about time.

Write your ideal week.

How many hours working?

How many hours learning?

How many hours exercising?

How many hours with family?

Now compare with current reality.

Money should support your ideal week, not sabotage it.

If you are earning high but constantly exhausted, something needs redesign.

Strategic Upgrades That Pay Back

Some expenses feel like spending but are actually investments.

Health

Nutritious food, gym membership, health checkups. Healthy body increases productivity.

Learning

Courses, books, workshops, mentorship. Skill upgrades increase earning potential.

Networking

Events, conferences, business meetups. Relationships create opportunities.

Tools

Laptop, software, workspace setup. Better tools increase output quality.

These expenses generate returns.

Differentiate between consumption and capacity-building.

Delayed Gratification Power

If you delay a purchase by 30 days and still want it, buy it.

Impulse purchases often fade after a week.

Create a “Pause Rule.”

Any non-essential expense above a certain amount must wait 7 to 30 days.

Example.

Rahul wanted to buy a ₹70,000 premium phone. Instead, he invested that amount into index funds. After three years at moderate growth, that investment became over ₹90,000.

Small delays compound over time.

The Freedom Ratio

Calculate how many months you can survive without income.

If your monthly expenses are ₹40,000 and you have ₹4,00,000 saved, you have 10 months of freedom.

As you increase savings and reduce unnecessary expenses, your freedom ratio increases.

High income with high expenses creates fragile life.

Moderate income with controlled expenses creates resilient life.

Designing Experiences Over Possessions

Research and observation consistently show experiences create longer-lasting happiness than material purchases.

Travel with friends.

Learning a new skill.

Starting a passion project.

Spending quality time with family.

Memories compound emotionally.

Possessions often lose excitement quickly.

Social Pressure and Spending

Many expenses are socially driven.

Branded clothing to impress.

Luxury car to signal success.

Expensive parties to fit in.

Ask yourself:

If no one could see this purchase, would I still buy it?

If the answer is no, reconsider.

Confidence is internal. Wealth signaling is external.

Building a Personal Spending Philosophy

Create three categories:

Non-Negotiable Joy

Expenses you deeply value and will never cut. Example: fitness, travel, family support.

Neutral Expenses

Necessary but not exciting. Optimize these.

Low-Value Expenses

Reduce or eliminate.

This philosophy prevents guilt while maintaining discipline.

Case Study: Designing a Balanced Life

Anita earned ₹1.2 lakh monthly. She felt constantly broke despite good income.

After mapping expenses, she realized:

₹25,000 monthly on food delivery and dining

₹10,000 on unused subscriptions

₹15,000 shopping

Happiness scores were low.

She reduced dining to ₹10,000. Cancelled subscriptions. Cut shopping by half.

She redirected ₹20,000 monthly into investments and ₹5,000 into weekend travel fund.

Within one year:

Her investments grew significantly.

She travelled six times.

Stress reduced.

Same income. Better design.

Money as a Tool, Not Master

Lifestyle design returns to the core mindset from Chapter One.

Money is a tool.

It can build health, relationships, learning, freedom.

Or it can trap you in comparison and endless consumption.

Your spending should reflect your values, not trends.

If you value creativity, spend on tools and learning.

If you value relationships, spend on shared experiences.

If you value independence, invest aggressively.

Balancing Enjoyment and Acceleration

You are building financial freedom before 30. That does not mean suffering through your twenties.

It means being intentional.

Save aggressively.

Invest consistently.

Spend consciously.

Avoid extremes of deprivation and reckless consumption.

Strategic living is about alignment.

The 48-Hour Reset Exercise

When you feel financially scattered:

Stop all non-essential spending for 48 hours.

Review accounts.

Check investment contributions.

Revisit goals.

Adjust budget if needed.

This simple reset restores control quickly.

Design Your Financial Identity

Are you someone who chases trends or someone who builds assets?

Are you reactive or intentional?

Lifestyle design is identity design.

Every purchase is a vote for the person you are becoming.

Spend like you mean it.

Spend aligned with goals.

Spend aligned with growth.

Spend aligned with freedom.

Because at the end, wealth is not just how much you accumulate.

It is how well your money supports the life you truly want.

The Investment Ladder: Real Estate, Stocks, and Passive Income

Climbing With Structure, Not Emotion

By now, you have built income, eliminated high-interest debt, automated savings, protected yourself with insurance, and designed your lifestyle intentionally.

Now comes the powerful stage: building assets that generate income and long-term wealth.

But here is the mistake most young earners make.

They jump into investments randomly.

One friend suggests stocks.

Another talks about crypto.

Family pushes real estate.

Without structure, investing becomes emotional gambling.

The Investment Ladder is a step-by-step progression. You climb one level at a time, increasing complexity and potential returns gradually.

This chapter will give you a practical entry-level playbook for stocks, real estate, and passive income streams.

Understanding the Ladder Concept

The ladder works like this:

Level One: Core Stock Market Investing

Level Two: Real Estate Exposure

Level Three: Scalable Passive Income Assets

Each level builds on previous stability.

You do not skip levels. You master one before climbing higher.

If you try advanced investments without strong foundation, risk increases unnecessarily.

Level One: Stocks as the Wealth Engine

For most people under 30, stocks should be the primary wealth-building tool.

Why?

Low entry barrier.

High liquidity.

Strong long-term growth potential.

Minimal operational involvement.

But the stock market is misunderstood.

It is not a place for daily trading for beginners. It is a system to own businesses over time.

Entry-Level Stock Market Playbook

Step One: Open Brokerage Account

Choose a low-cost broker. Ensure fees are transparent and minimal.

Step Two: Start With Index Funds

An index fund tracks a market index.

Instead of picking individual stocks, you buy a basket of top companies.

Why this works:

Diversification reduces risk.

No need to predict winners.

Historically strong long-term returns.

If you invest ₹15,000 monthly consistently into a broad market index fund for 10 years, compounding works quietly in your favor.

Step Three: Use SIP Strategy

Systematic Investment Plan means investing fixed amount every month automatically.

This reduces emotional timing mistakes.

When markets fall, your SIP buys more units. When markets rise, your investments grow.

Consistency beats prediction.

Basic Allocation Strategy

For someone under 30 with long-term horizon:

70 to 80 percent in diversified equity index funds

10 to 20 percent in safer debt instruments or bonds

Optional 5 to 10 percent in higher-risk ideas

This is a simple starting framework.

Adjust based on risk tolerance.

When to Buy Individual Stocks

Only after:

You understand company financials.

You can read basic income statements and balance sheets.

You are comfortable with volatility.

Limit individual stock exposure to small percentage initially.

Never invest money needed in next three to five years into equities.

Level Two: Real Estate as Stability Asset

Real estate creates psychological and financial stability.

But it requires capital, planning, and patience.

There are three main approaches.

Primary Residence

Buying a house to live in.

Advantages:

Emotional security.

Long-term appreciation potential.

Protection from rent inflation.

But do not rush into buying simply because others are.

Calculate:

EMI should not exceed 30 to 40 percent of monthly income.

Emergency fund must remain intact after down payment.

If buying property wipes out all savings, delay.

Rental Property

Buying property to rent out.

Entry-level checklist:

Rental yield calculation.

Location growth potential.

Maintenance cost estimation.

Vacancy risk consideration.

Example.

If property costs ₹50 lakh and generates ₹15,000 monthly rent, annual rent is ₹1.8 lakh.

Rental yield = 1.8 lakh divided by 50 lakh = 3.6 percent.

Compare this with alternative investments.

Real estate returns often come from appreciation plus rental income combined.

Real Estate Investment Trusts

For beginners without large capital, consider real estate investment trusts.

These allow small investment in commercial properties through stock exchange.

Benefits:

Lower entry cost.

Liquidity.

Passive exposure to property market.

This is often a good starting point before direct property ownership.

Level Three: Building Passive Income Assets

Passive income does not mean zero work. It means work once, earn multiple times.

Examples include:

Digital products

Online courses

Dividend-paying stocks

Rental property

Automated ecommerce systems

The goal is to create income streams not directly tied to hourly effort.

Dividend Investing

Certain companies distribute profits to shareholders as dividends.

If you own shares, you receive periodic payouts.

Dividend strategy works well when:

You reinvest dividends for growth in early years.

You focus on financially strong companies.

Do not chase high dividend percentage blindly. Stability matters more.

Digital Asset Example

Suppose you create a ₹999 online course.

If 500 people buy it over time, revenue becomes ₹4,99,500.

After initial effort, maintenance is minimal.

This transforms skill into scalable asset.

Similarly:

Templates.

Ebooks.

Subscription communities.

Digital leverage is powerful in your twenties.

The Risk Pyramid

Visualize your investments like a pyramid.

Base: Index funds and diversified equities

Middle: Real estate exposure

Top: High-risk ventures and startups

Never invert the pyramid.

Many young investors put 80 percent money in speculative assets. That is fragile.

Build foundation first.

The 10-Year Wealth Simulation

Let us look at an example.

At age 25, you invest ₹20,000 monthly in index funds with moderate annual growth.

In 10 years, you may accumulate significant corpus due to compounding.

Now imagine adding:

One rental property generating ₹20,000 monthly by age 32.

One digital asset generating ₹30,000 monthly.

Your total passive income becomes meaningful.

This is how wealth layers form.

Not overnight. Systematically.

When Markets Crash

Market downturns are normal.

If you have emergency fund and stable income, downturns become opportunity.

Continue SIP.

Avoid panic selling.

Review allocation but do not react emotionally.

Investing requires emotional discipline.

Asset Allocation Review

Once a year, review portfolio.

If equities have grown disproportionately, rebalance.

Rebalancing means selling small portion of overweight asset and allocating to underweight asset.

This maintains risk balance.

Common Mistakes to Avoid

Investing without emergency fund.

Taking loans to invest in volatile assets.

Following social media tips blindly.

Expecting quick returns.

Wealth building is a long game.

Case Study: Climbing the Ladder Correctly

Manish started investing ₹10,000 monthly at 24.

By 28, he increased to ₹25,000 monthly.

At 29, he bought small apartment with manageable EMI.

At 30, he launched a niche online course related to his profession.

By 33:

His equity investments compounded steadily.

Rental income covered part of EMI.

Course generated additional monthly income.

Multiple assets created resilience.

He did not chase trends. He climbed systematically.

The Power of Layered Income

Financial freedom before 30 does not mean you stop working.

It means your investments start contributing meaningfully to your expenses.

If your monthly expenses are ₹60,000 and your assets generate ₹25,000 passively, pressure reduces significantly.

Over time, that gap closes completely.

The Investor Identity

Shift identity from earner to owner.

When you invest, you become part-owner of businesses, properties, systems.

Ownership builds long-term security.

Earning is active. Ownership is strategic.

The ladder is clear.

Start with disciplined stock investing.

Add real estate wisely.

Build scalable passive income streams.

Do not rush. Do not gamble.

Climb step by step.

Your financial rocket now has multiple engines.

Income engine.

Investment engine.

Asset engine.

When all three work together, financial freedom stops being a dream.

It becomes a mathematical outcome.

Money and Relationships: Boundaries, Partners, and Career Moves

Why Money Conversations Shape Your Future

You can master investing, eliminate debt, and build income streams. But if you cannot handle money conversations with people around you, your financial life will feel unstable.

Money is emotional. It touches ego, status, fear, security, and identity.

Most conflicts in friendships, families, and marriages are not about money itself. They are about expectations, assumptions, and lack of communication.

Financial freedom before 30 is not only about numbers. It is about alignment.

In this chapter, you will learn how to create healthy money boundaries, communicate clearly with partners, manage family expectations, and make career moves without damaging relationships.

The Hidden Scripts We Carry

Every person grows up with a money script.

Some were taught:

Save every rupee.

Debt is dangerous.

Investing is risky.

Money is hard to earn.

Others were taught:

Money is for enjoyment.

Spend now, worry later.

Lifestyle shows success.

When two people with different scripts interact, friction happens.

First step is awareness.

Ask yourself:

What did I learn about money growing up?

Do I associate wealth with guilt or pride?

Do I fear discussing money?

Self-awareness reduces conflict.

Talking About Money With Friends

Friendships often break silently over money.

Splitting bills awkwardly.

Lending money without clarity.

Lifestyle differences creating pressure.

You must build boundaries early.

If a group plans expensive outings beyond your comfort, say:

"I am currently focusing on some financial goals, so I am being selective with spending. Let us plan something budget-friendly."

This communicates confidence, not scarcity.

True friends respect clarity.

If someone consistently pressures you to overspend, that is not financial alignment.

Lending Money to Friends

If you lend money, follow three rules.

Only lend what you can afford to lose.

Clarify repayment timeline clearly.

Avoid emotional expectations.

Example.

Instead of casually transferring ₹20,000, say:

"I can lend you ₹20,000. Let us agree on repayment in three monthly installments starting next month."

Clarity prevents resentment.

If you cannot afford to lend, say:

"I am not in a position to lend right now, but I hope things improve soon."

No explanation required.

Family Expectations and Boundaries

As income grows, family expectations may increase.

Support is noble. But unlimited obligation without planning creates stress.

Create a structured approach.

If you plan to contribute to family expenses, decide a fixed monthly amount.

Example.

You earn ₹80,000 monthly. You commit ₹15,000 monthly to family support. It becomes part of budget, not emotional reaction.

If relatives request money beyond your capacity, respond respectfully:

"I am currently committed to long-term financial goals and have limited flexibility. I hope you understand."

Boundaries are not disrespect. They are protection.

Discussing Money With a Partner

Money compatibility is as important as emotional compatibility.

Before marriage or long-term commitment, discuss:

Income levels

Debt status

Saving habits

Financial goals

Risk tolerance

Family responsibilities

Avoid assumptions.

Example questions:

What does financial security mean to you?

How much should we save monthly?

Are you comfortable with investments in stock market?

What is your view on taking loans?

Early conversations prevent later conflict.

Joint Versus Separate Finances

There is no universal rule. Choose based on comfort.

Common models include:

Fully Joint

All income pooled. All expenses shared.

Hybrid Model

Maintain joint account for common expenses. Keep personal accounts for individual spending.

Fully Separate

Each partner manages personal income and splits shared costs proportionally.

Hybrid model often works well for young couples.

Example.

If one partner earns ₹1,00,000 and the other ₹50,000, instead of splitting expenses 50-50, split proportionally.

This maintains fairness.

The Monthly Money Meeting

Schedule one financial review conversation monthly.

Agenda:

Review expenses.

Track investments.

Discuss upcoming major costs.

Align on goals.

Keep tone neutral. Focus on numbers, not blame.

Money meetings build trust.

Handling Income Differences

If one partner earns significantly more, ego or insecurity can appear.

The higher earner must avoid dominance.

The lower earner must avoid guilt.

Focus on teamwork.

Household contribution is not only financial. Emotional labor, household management, support all count.

Wealth building is partnership.

Career Moves and Relationship Impact

Changing careers, starting a business, or taking a pay cut affects everyone involved.

Before making a bold move, discuss:

How long income may reduce.

Emergency fund availability.

Worst-case scenario plan.

Example.

If you want to quit job and build startup, ensure:

At least six to twelve months of expenses saved.

Partner fully understands risk.

Clear milestone timeline defined.

Transparency builds support.

Surprises create fear.

When Values Clash

Sometimes financial values differ strongly.

One partner prioritizes luxury.

Other prioritizes aggressive investing.

Compromise through percentage allocation.

For example:

60 percent toward long-term goals.

20 percent toward lifestyle upgrades.

20 percent toward individual freedom spending.

Structure reduces emotional conflict.

Protecting Yourself Legally and Financially

If you enter business partnerships, document everything.

Profit sharing ratio.

Decision authority.

Exit conditions.

Even between close friends, written agreements prevent misunderstandings.

Trust plus clarity is stronger than trust alone.

Handling Social Comparison

In your twenties, social comparison intensifies.

Friends buying cars.

Colleagues traveling abroad.

Peers posting investment gains.

Remember:

You see their highlight reel, not their liabilities.

Comparison can push reckless decisions.

If a purchase is driven by comparison, pause.

Ask:

Is this aligned with my long-term plan?

Freedom requires discipline.

Money and Self-Worth

Do not attach identity to income level.

Income fluctuates.

Markets fluctuate.

Business revenue fluctuates.

Your value as person does not.

If you lose job or face temporary setback, communicate openly with partner and family.

Hiding financial problems increases damage.

Vulnerability builds trust.

Case Study: Financial Alignment Saved a Marriage

Ritesh was aggressive investor. His wife preferred savings in bank deposits.

Initially, conflicts were frequent.

Instead of arguing, they structured portfolio:

60 percent in diversified equity funds.

40 percent in safer instruments.

Both felt secure.

They scheduled monthly review sessions.

Five years later, their wealth grew steadily and conflict reduced drastically.

Alignment does not require identical thinking. It requires mutual respect.

The Confidence of Clear Boundaries

When you know your goals clearly, saying no becomes easier.

No to unnecessary loans.

No to overspending.

No to risky joint ventures.

Boundaries protect relationships.

People respect clarity more than silent resentment.

Building a Financially Healthy Social Circle

Surround yourself with people who:

Discuss growth.

Respect financial discipline.

Encourage learning and investing.

Environment influences spending habits and ambition levels.

Choose wisely.

Money as a Shared Vision

Money conversations should not feel like conflict.

They should feel like planning a shared future.

Financial freedom before 30 is powerful.

But shared freedom is stronger.

When partners align, friends respect boundaries, and family expectations are structured, money becomes a tool of stability instead of stress.

Your financial rocket does not travel alone.

It travels with people around you.

Choose communication over assumption.

Choose clarity over avoidance.

Choose boundaries over silent sacrifice.

Because strong relationships combined with strong finances create a life that is not only wealthy, but deeply secure.

Launch Your Freedom Plan: 5-Year Path to Financial Independence

The Moment of Commitment

You have reached the final chapter.

You now understand mindset, cash flow, debt elimination, automation, investing, scaling income, lifestyle design, and relationship alignment.

But knowledge alone does not create freedom.

Execution does.

This chapter is your launch sequence.

It is a practical five-year roadmap designed for someone starting in their early or mid-twenties who wants financial independence before 30 or shortly after.

Financial independence does not mean you stop working.

It means your assets generate enough income to cover your core expenses.

It means you work because you choose to, not because you are forced to.

Now we build that outcome step by step.

Define Financial Independence Clearly

Before designing a five-year plan, define your number.

Step One: Calculate Monthly Freedom Expense

List essential living costs:

Housing

Food

Utilities

Transport

Insurance

Basic lifestyle

Example:

Rent: ₹20,000

Food: ₹10,000

Utilities: ₹5,000

Transport: ₹5,000

Insurance: ₹3,000

Miscellaneous essentials: ₹7,000

Total: ₹50,000 per month

Annual requirement: ₹6,00,000

Step Two: Estimate Required Corpus

If you assume a safe withdrawal rate around 4 to 5 percent annually, you can calculate approximate target corpus.

₹6,00,000 divided by 0.04 equals ₹1.5 crore.

That becomes your financial independence number.

Your number may vary.

But clarity transforms dream into measurable goal.

Year One: Stabilize and Build Foundation

Primary focus: Control and clarity.

Actions:

Eliminate all high-interest debt.

Build three to six months emergency fund.

Automate savings and investments.

Start monthly SIP in diversified index funds.

Learn one high-income skill.

Target by end of Year One:

Net worth positive.

At least 20 to 30 percent of income invested monthly.

Emergency fund fully funded.

If you start with ₹0 net worth and save ₹20,000 monthly, you accumulate ₹2.4 lakh in one year excluding growth.

Momentum begins here.

Year Two: Increase Income Aggressively

Primary focus: Expansion.

Your biggest advantage in your twenties is earning potential.

Actions:

Negotiate salary increment.

Switch job if necessary for growth.

Monetize skill through freelancing.

Increase investment percentage with income growth.

Example:

If salary increases from ₹50,000 to ₹70,000, maintain old lifestyle and invest difference.

If you add ₹25,000 monthly through freelance or business, your annual investment capacity increases dramatically.

Target by end of Year Two:

Investing at least 35 to 40 percent of income.

Side income contributing minimum 20 percent of total income.

Net worth potentially reaching ₹6 to ₹10 lakh depending on starting point.

Income acceleration compresses timeline.

Year Three: Build Assets Beyond Salary

Primary focus: Asset diversification.

Actions:

Increase SIP amount systematically.

Consider real estate exposure if financially stable.

Build one scalable income asset such as digital product or small business system.

Reinvest profits aggressively.

If your annual investment reaches ₹6 to ₹8 lakh and grows steadily, compounding starts becoming visible.

Example:

Suppose by Year Three your portfolio reaches ₹15 lakh. With disciplined investing and moderate growth, acceleration becomes noticeable.

This is also the stage where many people lose discipline due to lifestyle upgrades.

Stay focused.

Year Four: Optimize and Scale

Primary focus: Efficiency and leverage.

By now, you should have:

Stable income streams.

Emergency buffer intact.

Investment habit ingrained.

Actions:

Rebalance portfolio annually.

Reduce unnecessary expenses further.

Expand side business into structured small enterprise if viable.

Increase passive income streams.

If your side business generates ₹50,000 monthly and investments generate growing returns, psychological shift occurs.

You begin to feel control.

Target by end of Year Four:

Net worth reaching 50 to 70 percent of independence target depending on income trajectory.

This stage demands patience. Do not rush risky investments.

Year Five: Acceleration Toward Independence

Primary focus: Convergence.

By Year Five, if executed consistently:

Your investment corpus may approach significant milestone.

Your passive income streams may cover 30 to 60 percent of expenses.

Actions:

Increase investments with any windfall.

Avoid lifestyle inflation spikes.

Review independence number and adjust for inflation.

Consider reducing work hours if passive income strong.

If your required annual expense is ₹6 lakh and passive income reaches ₹3 lakh annually, you are halfway free.

Halfway freedom already changes mindset.

Net Worth Milestones and Actions

Milestone One: First ₹1 Lakh

Focus on habit formation.

Celebrate discipline, not amount.

Action:

Continue automation. Avoid complacency.

Milestone Two: ₹5 Lakh

Momentum phase.

Action:

Increase SIP. Explore additional asset classes cautiously.

Milestone Three: ₹10 Lakh

Serious investor stage.

Action:

Review allocation strategy. Ensure diversification. Consider tax optimization.

Milestone Four: ₹25 Lakh

Acceleration visible.

Action:

Evaluate real estate opportunity if aligned. Expand scalable income.

Milestone Five: ₹50 Lakh

Confidence zone.

Action:

Shift some focus toward capital preservation along with growth. Strengthen passive streams.

Milestone Six: ₹1 Crore and Beyond

Strategic wealth stage.

Action:

Focus on sustainability, risk management, and life design.

At this level, small percentage returns create large absolute growth.

The Mathematics of Consistency

Let us simulate.

If you invest ₹30,000 monthly with moderate annual growth over five years, you accumulate meaningful corpus.

If you increase to ₹50,000 monthly by Year Three, growth accelerates dramatically.

The key variable is not stock picking.

It is contribution rate.

Increase income.

Control expenses.

Invest difference.

Repeat.

What If You Start Late

If you begin at 27 or 28, compress timeline through:

Higher savings rate.

Aggressive income scaling.

Temporary lifestyle sacrifice.

Even saving 50 percent of income for five years creates powerful shift.

Financial freedom is not age-dependent. It is discipline-dependent.

Handling Setbacks

Market crash.

Job loss.

Business failure.

These will happen.

Your emergency fund protects you.

Your diversified investments reduce risk.

Your skill stack protects income.

Do not abandon plan due to temporary setback.

Adjust. Continue.

Quarterly Freedom Checkpoints

Every three months:

Calculate net worth.

Review investment contributions.

Track passive income growth.

Evaluate expense creep.

Small corrections prevent large deviations.

The 50 Percent Rule

When your investments generate 50 percent of your monthly expenses passively, psychological freedom begins.

At this stage you can:

Negotiate job more confidently.

Reduce toxic work exposure.

Take calculated entrepreneurial risks.

Financial independence is gradual, not sudden.

Designing Post-Independence Life

What will you do when you reach independence?

Start business?

Travel?

Work part-time?

Mentor others?

Freedom without purpose creates emptiness.

Define purpose before arrival.

The Identity Shift

You began as consumer.

You became saver.

You evolved into investor.

Now you become asset builder.

This identity shift is the true transformation.

Once you see money as tool to buy time, your decisions change permanently.

Five-Year Example Case

Let us consider a realistic example.

Age 25. Income ₹60,000 monthly.

Year One:

Saves ₹20,000 monthly. Builds ₹2.4 lakh plus emergency fund.

Year Two:

Income increases to ₹80,000. Saves ₹35,000 monthly. Adds freelance income ₹15,000.

Total annual investment crosses ₹6 lakh.

Year Three:

Investment corpus approaches ₹15 to ₹20 lakh with growth. Launches small digital product generating ₹20,000 monthly.

Year Four:

Total monthly investment reaches ₹50,000. Business income rises to ₹40,000 monthly.

Year Five:

Corpus approaches ₹40 to ₹60 lakh range depending on returns. Passive income meaningful portion of expenses.

This person may not be fully independent yet, but trajectory is powerful.

Another five years at same pace may close gap entirely.

The difference between average and free is not intelligence.

It is consistency.

The Discipline Advantage

Most people quit after one year.

Some slow down after three years.

Very few continue five years without interruption.

If you commit fully to five-year plan, you already outperform majority.

Freedom favors disciplined minority.

Rules for the Journey

Increase income every year.

Invest before spending.

Avoid high-interest debt permanently.

Protect with insurance and buffer.

Track net worth quarterly.

Design lifestyle intentionally.

These rules compound.

Your Personal Freedom Blueprint

Write down:

Current net worth.

Monthly savings rate.

Target corpus.

Five-year projected corpus if consistent.

Now reverse engineer required monthly investment.

Break it into monthly actions.

Do not overcomplicate.

Numbers create clarity.

The Emotional Reward

When you check your investments and see steady growth, anxiety reduces.

When passive income hits your account, confidence rises.

When you realize you could survive months without salary, fear disappears.

That emotional freedom is priceless.

The Final Launch

Financial freedom is not magic.

It is mathematics plus discipline plus patience.

You have the tools.

You have the roadmap.

You have the strategy.

Now you need the decision.

Five years will pass anyway.

The only question is:

Will you arrive there financially constrained or financially free?

Start today.

Automate the first investment.

Increase the first income stream.

Track the first milestone.

Climb steadily.

Your financial rocket is built.

The countdown has begun.

Five.

Four.

Three.

Two.

One.

Launch.

www.ingramcontent.com/pod-product-compliance
Lightning Source LLC
La Vergne TN
LVHW022112200926
848481LV00003B/1147
* 9 7 9 8 2 3 2 2 8 6 1 0 1 *